Discover the Tudors

Elizabeth I

Moira Butterfield

W
FRANKLIN WATTS

This edition published in 2013 by Franklin Watts

Copyright © Franklin Watts 2013

Franklin Watts
338 Euston Road
London NW1 3BH

Franklin Watts Australia
Level 17/207 Kent Street
Sydney NSW 2000

A CIP catalogue record for this book
is available from the British Library.

Dewey number: 942.05'2'092

ISBN 978 1 4451 1856 7

Printed in China

Franklin Watts is a division of Hachette Children's Books,
an Hachette UK company

www.hachette.co.uk

Designer: Jason Billin
Editor: Sarah Ridley
Art Director: Jonathan Hair
Editor-in-Chief: John C. Miles
Picture research: Diana Morris

Contents

The Lady Princess

On Sunday 7 September, 1533, Princess Elizabeth Tudor was born at Greenwich Palace, near London.

A disappointing baby

Elizabeth's parents were Henry VIII and his second wife Anne Boleyn. Henry was disappointed at the birth of a girl. He had longed for a boy who would become king after his death, and was worried that other nobles would try to steal the crown if there was not a male heir. He already had one daughter, Mary, born to his first wife Catherine of Aragon.

Rejecting Rome

When Henry fell in love with Anne Boleyn, he had to ask the Pope for permission to divorce Catherine. The Pope was the head of the Roman Catholic Church, England's religion at the time. When the Pope said no, Henry declared himself head of a new church – the Church of England – so he could divorce without the Pope's agreement. This led to years of religious unrest in the country.

Elizabeth's father, Henry VIII.

The young princess

Elizabeth was known as "The Lady Princess", and she spent her early years at Hatfield House (below). When she was only two years old, her mother was charged with being unfaithful to the King, imprisoned in the Tower of London and executed (put to death). Elizabeth never spoke or wrote about this dreadful event in her life.

Elizabeth's mother Anne Boleyn. Henry VIII had her executed.

Elizabeth spent most of her young life at Hatfield House.

Go and visit

Hatfield House is about 30 kilometres north of London. An oak tree outside is said to mark the place where Elizabeth was standing when she first heard she was to be Queen.

A clever girl

In May 1536 Henry married his third wife, Jane Seymour, and Elizabeth's life changed once more.

A new brother

Elizabeth was a bright and charming little girl, looked after by nannies. In October 1537 she got a new half-brother when Jane Seymour gave birth to a son called Edward. Sadly Jane died a couple of weeks later. Elizabeth loved Edward and they sometimes shared lessons together. They had the best tutors (teachers) in the land, and they were both said to be clever young scholars.

A portrait of Elizabeth at about the age of 13.

Elizabeth's half-brother Edward, whom she adored.

Faraway father

Elizabeth loved her father dearly but she hardly ever saw him. On one unusual occasion in 1542 Henry had dinner with his daughters, Mary and Elizabeth, and was said to be very impressed with his girls, particularly Elizabeth. She had the same colouring as him, with red-gold hair and pale skin. She tried to get on as best she could with her sister Mary, but Mary was much older than her, and a devout Roman Catholic. She suspected Elizabeth of secretly being a Protestant.

A life in danger

Henry VIII died in 1547, and Elizabeth's ten-year-old brother was crowned Edward VI of England.

A dangerous death

Edward was a Protestant, and during his short reign Catholics were imprisoned and executed. Then, in 1553, Edward died at the age of 16 and Mary was crowned Queen, determined to make England Roman Catholic again. Elizabeth feared for her life and tried to keep away from court.

The Wyatt Rebellion

Mary was desperate to marry and give birth to a Catholic heir. In 1554 she was set to marry the devout Catholic King Philip II of Spain, so Protestants decided

Key fact

In Tudor times people took religion very seriously. All over Europe, people argued about the right way to worship God. Roman Catholics followed the leadership and teachings of the Pope in Rome but Protestants held different Christian beliefs, first set out by a German monk called Martin Luther.

Queen Mary I, who imprisoned Elizabeth in the Tower of London.

it was time to act against her. Sir Thomas Wyatt and his followers hatched a plot to get rid of her but it failed and the plotters were executed. Mary was sure that Elizabeth was connected to the plot, and she ordered her sister to be arrested. Elizabeth was kept in the Tower of London for nearly three months. She feared her life was over, but eventually she was released without any charge.

Long live the Queen

Mary died childless in 1558 and Elizabeth was declared Queen, aged 25.

First impressions

Elizabeth was in the park at Hatfield House when she heard the news of her sister's death. As she was presented with Mary's ring she knelt down and said in Latin:

"God has done it and it is marvellous in our eyes!"

A few days later she appeared before her royal advisors in the Great Hall at Hatfield (right) and made her first speech. She came to London a couple of days later, part of a street procession (parade) of over a thousand nobles riding on horseback.

The Queen's people

Elizabeth made Sir William Cecil her chief minister, and he stayed as her loyal advisor for the next 40 years. During the early part of her reign, one of her closest friends and advisors was Robert Dudley, Earl of Leicester. Some people even thought they were secretly in love.

Key fact

Elizabeth was strict with her court and hated being disobeyed. Nobody was allowed to sit while she stood, and anyone who met the Queen and wished to speak to her had to do it on bended knee.

The Great Hall at
Hatfield House

A magnificent coronation

Elizabeth was crowned Queen at a magnificent ceremony on 15 January, 1559.

Long Live the Queen!

Elizabeth made sure that her coronation looked very grand. She wanted to show people that she was the rightful heir to the throne, and she wanted everyone to think this was the beginning of a wonderful new age.

Kind lady

Celebrations began on the eve of the coronation. Elizabeth was paraded through the streets, stopping to give kind words to the elderly and poor and accepting posies of flowers from children.

A portrait of Elizabeth with the orb and sceptre.

A great day

The next day Elizabeth was crowned in Westminster Abbey. She was anointed (rubbed) with holy oil, the crown was placed on her head and she was handed an orb and sceptre – symbols of the monarch's power. Later there was a banquet that lasted for ten hours.

In the Rainbow Portrait *of 1600 (right) the Queen's clothes are decorated with eyes and ears to suggest that she sees and hears everything.*

Key fact

Elizabeth believed that how she looked was important. Her clothes and jewels were carefully chosen to make her stand out. Sometimes it took two hours or more for her servants to get her dressed.

The Queen means business

Elizabeth was eager to get down to the serious business of ruling the country.

I'm in charge

The opening of Parliament took place on 25 January 1559 and the new Queen immediately made her mark. She made it clear she would not be told what to do and she had total power over the country, even though she was a woman. Each day she set a time for discussing government business and meeting with her advisors. She knew this was important because she had many problems to deal with, including a country that was divided over religion.

Go to Church

Elizabeth was Protestant and she was keen to reform (change) the Church, but she did not want to make enemies of the Catholics. In matters of religion she wanted to take "a middle way". In May 1559 the Church of England became established by law, and those who refused to attend church on Sunday could be fined.

Key fact

Elizabeth had inherited big debts from her father and sister. During her reign she managed to pay back this money by raising taxes, selling off land and being careful what she spent.

ELIZABETH · · REGINA ·

The young queen – a portrait painted in the early 1560s.

Who will be King?

Elizabeth came under pressure to marry and have children to succeed her to the throne.

Marry me

During the first months of her reign Elizabeth received offers of marriage from monarchs around Europe, but she said no to everyone. When her marriage was discussed in Parliament she got annoyed, and said:

"I am already bound unto a husband, which is the kingdom of England."

Key fact

Many Catholics believed that Elizabeth's cousin, Mary Queen of Scots, was the rightful Queen of England. There was always a danger that they would try to depose (get rid) of Elizabeth and put Mary on the throne, especially as Elizabeth had no children to succeed (rule after) her.

A secret scandal

Elizabeth was close to a nobleman called Robert Dudley, and she made him Earl of Leicester. Many people thought she would like to marry him but he already had a wife. His wife died in 1560 by falling down the stairs, and there were rumours that Dudley had ordered her murder. This harmful gossip meant that Elizabeth could never

A painting that shows Elizabeth and Robert Dudley enjoying a royal picnic.

marry Dudley without damaging her reputation (what people thought about her).

Single and strong

In Tudor times some people thought that a woman was too weak to rule, but Elizabeth proved them wrong. Perhaps she preferred not to share the throne with anyone because people would probably have treated her husband as the ruler, not her.

Elizabeth's favourite, Robert Dudley. She admired his hunting, dancing and many other skills.

England's splendid houses

When she came to the throne, Elizabeth inherited about 60 palaces and houses.

A choice of palaces

The main Tudor palaces were around London, on the banks of the River Thames. Whitehall Palace, in the centre of London, was Elizabeth's main winter home and had over 2,000 rooms. It was one of the biggest palaces in Europe, but it burnt down in the 17th century.

Hampton Court, one of the royal palaces on the Thames.

On tour

In summer Elizabeth often went on a grand tour of her royal palaces and the homes of her courtiers. Usually, she travelled in an open carriage so that ordinary people could see her. Streams of courtiers rode behind her.

Hardwick Hall in Derbyshire, a good example of a grand Elizabethan house.

Expensive guests

During Elizabeth's reign many fine country houses were built by her courtiers. If the Queen came to visit, her nobles were expected to spare no expense entertaining her. Her visits were very costly, because her entire court came with her and everybody had to be housed and fed. William Cecil, who became Lord Burghley, even built extra rooms and created gardens for the Queen at his home, Burghley House.

Go and visit

Elizabeth gave Kenilworth Castle in Warwickshire (below) to Robert Dudley in 1563. He made it one of the grandest homes in England, and Elizabeth visited many times. In 1575 she stayed for ten days and was treated to torch-lit dinners, music and fireworks.

Life at the Royal Court

Elizabeth always had the Royal Court around her, made up of hundreds of nobles and servants.

Be careful of the Queen

Life at court was exciting but it was competitive too, as people tried to outdo each other to please the Queen. If someone upset her, she could ban them from court in disgrace. She liked to stay up late at night and slept late in the mornings, and was always attended by her ladies-in-waiting – noblewomen who acted as her personal maids.

Poetry for the Queen

The Queen enjoyed poetry, too. In 1589 the poet Edmund Spenser dedicated his long poem *The Faerie Queen* to her, and in return he was given a pension (a regular payment). The poem was full of compliments to Elizabeth.

By Royal command

Visitors, such as foreign ambassadors, often arrived at court and Elizabeth liked to impress them with banquets, music and acting performances. Plays by William Shakespeare and Ben Jonson were performed before the Queen and her courtiers. Shakespeare is believed to have written *The Merry Wives of Windsor* and *Twelfth Night* especially for her. With her support, plays became popular and public theatres opened in London, including Shakespeare's Globe Theatre.

Go and visit

Shakespeare's Globe Theatre (below) has been recreated close to its original site in London. Plays are performed there in the summer.

Plots against the Queen

Mary Queen of Scots was a serious threat to Elizabeth because her Catholic supporters wanted her on the throne.

Troublesome cousin

Mary grew up in France and married the French king in 1558. She came back to Scotland when the King died, and married a Scottish nobleman called Lord Darnley. In 1566 she had a son, James, the heir to the Scottish throne. In 1567 Darnley was murdered and Mary married the Earl of Bothwell, believed to be his murderer. The scandal forced her to give up her throne, and she fled to England.

This medal commemorates the marriage of Mary Queen of Scots to Henry, Lord Darnley.

Catholic rebellion

Elizabeth kept Mary under house arrest for the next 19 years and planted spies in her house to try to discover any plans to steal the throne. During that time there were several Catholic-backed attempts to overthrow

Elizabeth and put Mary on the throne, but there was no proof that Mary herself was involved. Elizabeth had to start taking a hard line with Catholics, executing those suspected of plotting against her.

Mary found guilty

In 1585 Mary was finally caught plotting against Elizabeth, supported by Philip II of Spain. Elizabeth did not want her cousin to be executed but Parliament convinced her there was no other way. On 8 February, 1587, Mary Queen of Scots was beheaded.

Mary Queen of Scots.

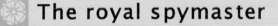

The royal spymaster

Sir Francis Walsingham was Elizabeth's spymaster. He placed about 50 undercover agents in the royal courts of Europe, to find out if there was any plotting against her. It was Walsingham's spies who finally discovered Mary plotting to take the throne.

Elizabeth at war

Elizabeth tried to avoid war, but sometimes she acted to weaken other countries.

The Queen's pirates

Catholic Philip II of Spain was Elizabeth's main enemy. Spain had colonies in the New World (America), and Elizabeth saw her chance to weaken the Spanish there and to increase her own country's wealth.

This painting shows Elizabeth visiting troops at Tilbury in 1588. She gave a famous speech:

"I am come amongst you not for my recreation and disport, but being resolved in the midst and heat of the battle to live or die amongst you all."

She sent English sailors, like Sir Francis Drake, to steal treasure from Spanish ships.

The Armada

In the summer of 1588 Philip sent a fleet of 130 Spanish ships, carrying 30,000 men and 2,500 guns. The fleet was called the Armada and the plan was to invade England, put Philip II's daughter on the throne and make England Roman Catholic once more.

Victory at sea

Elizabeth was ready for war because her spies had predicted it. She had an army of about 20,000 men gathered at Tilbury in Essex and a fleet of 150 ships waiting at Plymouth. On 9 August she visited the troops at Tilbury and made a famous speech (see opposite). The English navy defeated the mighty Armada, helped by storms that scattered the Spanish ships.

The Armada Jewel, made to celebrate the victory and given as a gift by Elizabeth to a loyal advisor.

The end of the Earl

Elizabeth's happiness after defeating the Armada was short-lived. Robert Dudley, Earl of Leicester, died on 4 September 1588, and the Queen was grief-stricken. She kept his last letter to her by her bedside, where it was found when she died many years later.

High days and dark days

Victory over the Armada turned Elizabeth into one of the most powerful monarchs of her time.

More respect

By defeating the Spanish, Elizabeth brought more stability at home. Roman Catholics and Protestants were united in their respect for her and the Church of England became stronger. By now she was 55 years old, and even though she was fit and healthy, many of her old friends and advisors began to die.

Elizabeth's courtiers carry her in a litter at the wedding of a noble in 1600. The bride stands behind the litter in her white dress.

Elizabeth didn't like being ill and often refused to take medicine or see a doctor.

As she grew older she suffered from terrible toothache but refused to have her teeth pulled out. Towards the end of her life her eyes began to fail and she lost her memory.

Elizabeth in her later years. The figures behind her represent Time (left) and Death.

A favourite falls

For a while Robert Devereux, Earl of Essex, became the Queen's favourite. They did everything together and she gave him political power. But eventually his thirst for more power led him to rebel against the Queen, and he was executed in 1601.

Problems never stop

Elizabeth never had a peaceful problem-free time. The threat of a Spanish invasion never went away and she had to put up taxes to pay for more defences. In parts of the country the increased taxes caused riots. Then in the 1590s the harvests failed and famine (starvation) affected many people.

End of an era

After Essex was executed the Queen grew more unhappy and had less time for the business of government.

Time to go

In the later years of Elizabeth's reign there was more unrest on the streets, and people began to suggest that the Queen might be too old to deal with the country's problems. She began writing to James VI of Scotland, the son of Mary Queen of Scots, but she kept refusing to name him as her successor.

A final naming

When Elizabeth caught a fever in March 1603, her advisors begged her to name her successor. At the end she could barely speak but made it known that James VI of Scotland was her choice. She died on 24 March, 1603.

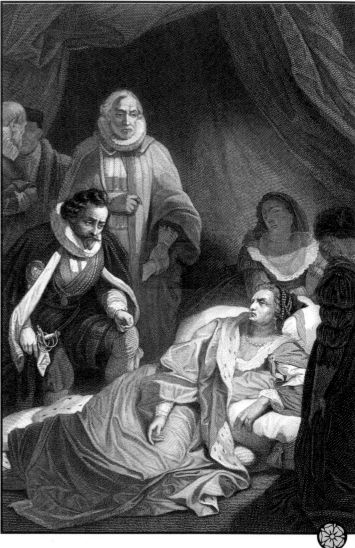

A 19th-century impression of Elizabeth's death at Richmond Palace.

Elizabeth's funeral procession makes its way to Westminster Abbey.

Funeral for a Queen

Elizabeth's coffin was sailed downriver from Richmond on a torchlit barge, then carried to Westminster Abbey on a hearse drawn by horses draped in black velvet. She was remembered as a Queen who brought peace and prosperity to England, and in the years after her death she became known as "Good Queen Bess". With her death the era of the Tudors ended, and the reign of the Stuarts began.

Go and visit

Elizabeth is buried in the beautiful Henry VII Chapel at Westminster Abbey, sharing the same tomb as her sister Mary Tudor, opposite the tomb of her cousin, Mary Queen of Scots.

Glossary

ambassador
A person sent to a foreign country on official business.

Armada
A fleet of Spanish ships sent to invade England.

banquet
A celebration meal for a large number of people.

coronation
Official crowning of a King or Queen.

court
Advisors and nobles who attend the monarch.

courtier
A person who attends the court.

devout
Deeply religious.

heir
Someone who will be given money, property or a title when somebody else dies.

house arrest
Imprisonment in your home, rather than in a prison.

inherit
To get money, property or a title from somebody who has died.

lady-in-waiting
A lady companion to a queen or princess.

litter
A seat fitted to a platform that can be carried along by servants.

monarch
A King or Queen.

parliament
Group of officials who pass the country's laws.

Protestantism
A Christian religion rejecting the authority of the Pope.

Roman Catholicism
A Christian religion led by the Pope.

successor
The person who will take over a position from somebody else.

suitor
A man who wants to marry a particular woman.

treason
The crime of betraying your country or plotting against the King or Queen.

Timeline

1533 Elizabeth is born at Greenwich Palace, London.

1536 Anne Boleyn is executed.

1547 Henry VIII dies.

1553 Edward VI dies and is succeeded by Mary I.

1558 Mary I dies and is succeeded by Elizabeth.

1559 Elizabeth's coronation ceremony.

1568 Mary Queen of Scots flees to England and is imprisoned by Elizabeth.

1575 Robert Dudley entertains Elizabeth at Kenilworth Castle.

1577–1580 Francis Drake sails around the world.

1580 Pope Gregory XIII announces that killing Elizabeth is not a sin.

1586 Babington Plot to overthrow Elizabeth is uncovered.

1587 Mary Queen of Scots is executed.

1588 Launch and defeat of Philip II of Spain's Armada.

1588 Robert Dudley dies.

1590 Sir Francis Walsingham dies.

1598 Lord Burghley (William Cecil) dies.

1601 Robert Devereux, Earl of Essex, is executed for treason.

1603 Queen Elizabeth I dies and is succeeded by James VI of Scotland who becomes James I.

Websites

http://tudorhistory.org/elizabeth/
An interesting biography of Elizabeth I with lots of contemporary paintings.

www.historylearningsite.co.uk/ elizabeth_i.htm
A good place to learn about Elizabeth and all the other Tudor monarchs.

www.bbc.co.uk/schools/ primaryhistory/famouspeople/ elizabeth_i/
A great site for children, packed with information, fun facts, a visual timeline of the Tudors, photos and videos.

www.snaithprimary.eril.net/ ttss.html
A lively site prepared especially for schoolchildren. Lots of interesting activities.

http://www.tudorbritain.org/
A fabulous site for children learning about Elizabeth and the Tudors, created by the Victoria and Albert Museum, London.

Index